19 <u>95</u>

POETRY IN THE GARDEN

WE TOO WILL HAVE A GARDEN SOME DAY

POETRY IN THE GARDEN

Edited by
Jacqueline Miller Bachar

International Forum
Palos Verdes Peninsula, California
1996

Please direct all correspondence and book orders to:

International Forum
P.O.Box 7000-350
Palos Verdes Peninsula, CA 90274

Library of Congress Catalog Number 96-75021

Book and Cover Design by White Light Publishing.

Cover illustration—Antique trading card from the editor's private collection of 19th century ephemera

Printed in the United States of America

ISBN 1-886934-07-x

$\mathcal{F}$or my husband Paul

Acknowledgements

I wish to thank those California women whose work is included in this book, and whose love of nature and concepts of garden is expressed in such special ways.

Thanks to those unknown artists whose charming works are used to illustrate this book. They are from my private collection of antique ephemera dating from the late 1800's to 1907.

Special thanks to my husband Paul and Virginia Twohy for their editing skills.

—Jacqueline Bachar, Editor

*L*ist of Illustrations

Contents

Buddha

Susan Salomon Neiman

Buddha watches me
Peeking through blue flowers
Smiling as I weed
Curling vines from his feet
Covering his lotus legs.
He winks at the fluttering hummingbird
Sucking white blossoms from the kumquat tree.
I touch sun-warmed stone
His hands open
My sweat drips
on his now bare lap.

Solidly he sits
contemplating tangerines growing
Golden koi dancing
Under yellow water lilies.
Bumble bees buzzing
Crawling lizards creeping snails
Mourning doves swooping jays
Anemone narcissus wild indigo
Amaryllis tuberose
Sunflower of my heart
Seeing through closed eyes.

૭૭

An Unseen Admirer

Susan Norton

Sitting at my kitchen window,
Watching the wind amble through my garden,
Every leaf and petal gently fondled,
None ignored
Each felt adored
        cherished
              special
What a marvel!
What power—
In the appreciating touch of an unseen admirer.

℗

Dream 2

Carol Soucek King

Golden hair and shimmering rays
On glistening gems mid our creek's run
My little girl is lost in play—
By gathering stones, she holds the sun!

Vertical spires of green surround
No man-made object on this spot.
Only my child lost in play,
A child attuned to her soul today.

Hallowed moment, oh sylvan scene
of daughter entranced by garden's gleam,
Nurturing every future year
By being at one with nature here.

Intimate feelings beyond compare
of understanding her one-ness there
Can help forever the human race—
A child aware of garden's grace!

❧

Summer Kingdom

June Reames

I survey my kingdom from a knotted throne.
Above, tall oaks gently tear the sunshine
    into golden drops of summer rain,
splashing below into brilliant puddles of light.
The cool breeze carries the gossip and laughter of
feathered Lords and Ladies bedecked in rainbow hues.
Before me perform the court jesters of my kingdom.
Squirrels and chipmunks trade jokes and scamper off
    at the arrival of my Prime Minister.
Dressed in gray, he strolls with feline grace to my throne,
    then leaps into my lap purring a greeting—
Evening softly arrives.
Stars and fireflies turn my kingdom into an enchanted glade
    befitting royalty.
A voice calls from the house reminding me that my kingdom is
my backyard, my throne a gently swaying hammock.
I must leave my kingdom for the night.
As I go, I call a soft farewell to the many denizens of my
    summer kingdom.

છ

An Inheritance

Ruth Adams

My mother and I lived with her mother in a household of women:
widow, spinster aunt, divorcee and child.
A garden of women.

Behind the house wedged into its small city lot were tomatoes.
Always tomatoes. Sometimes giant sunflowers. Feverfew.
A few rows of corn.
But always tomatoes, sweet alyssum for the birds and roses.

Summer afternoons when tomatoes glowed ripe,
Mama grabbed a saltshaker.
We went into the garden, she and I.
We stood among the vines munching salty tomatoes sweet and
warm from the sun and watched Grandma tend her roses.

She trod softly, carefully between the plants washing aphids
from each leaf and stem and bud with soapsuds.
In her pail soapsuds glistened with tiny rainbows.
Her hair was a silver halo in the sun.

That garden and its women are long, long gone but
among my fancy hybrids blooms one modest shell-pink tea-rose.
Grandma, when we left that home behind, cut a slip.
It burgeoned so that Mama slipped it once again and grew it in
another garden where it flourished until I,
establishing my own, began with that self-same rose.

Sometimes I grow sunflowers. Feverfew.
A few rows of corn.
But always tomatoes, sweet alyssum for the birds and roses.

✌

Flowers of Earth

Emily Greenstadt

Lilacs bloom in early April.
Bees collect nectar from an endless line of clover.
Lily stems stand green and tall.
Mint leaves dangle, overdosed with color.
Rose petals caress like silk.
Lotus blossom centers shine bold as the sun.
All dazzling to our eyes.

Flowers…
The beginning of life.

෴

Manna

Barbara Kovner

A
tall
tree
spread
its needled
branches casting
shadows over the small
square of earth where she
planted flower seeds in May
yellow pollen sifts down from
cones dusting thrusting leaves
with gold summer's fierce sun
shrivels thirsty buds
she spreads the opened
paper parasol in her garden's
center her watering can sprays
cooling spurts onto waiting leaves
at six she had not yet learned
the basics of balance
dark and light
night and day
hot and cold
wet and dry
yin * yang

෴

Weeds

Lois Olsen

It was damn hot, and there I was
nesting in amongst the weeds,
squatting low, admiring their tenacity.
The miracle of their survival.
Turgidus weeds, breaking through sidewalks,
cracking the patio pavement,
piercing the most desolate corner to find the light.
Where there's a weed there's a way.

১

Sanctuary

Marilyn Norma Limond

Driftwood forests and gardens
flourish in salt air.
Bleached by the sun,
their gray-white limbs
are bare of leaves.
Seabirds play in their branches,
rest on the blunt ends,
call it home.

❧

The Spider Plant

Yetta Speevack

That summer rain forgot New York
My spider plant languished on the fire escape
Without any manna from heaven
While I flew to distant countries.

> Seven weeks of drought
> Hardy plant, can you survive?

My solace your sturdy stamina
At home in fields and city houses
Covering the ground with leafy green
Swinging high in hanging baskets.

I miss your green white blades
Draped like a crown around the pot
Stems bearing little white flowers
Magically becoming mother plants.

Like a spider you climb into nearby pots
Seek soil to anchor your rooted shoots
Birthing striated babies along the way
While you purify the air.

Home, I dread to find you dead
You look gray and droopy. But, oh delight!
I discover sparks of life. Pour pitchers of water
You drink and drink to quench your great thirst.

I wash each tender blade. Loosen the soil
Turn you to the sun. Whisper, "I missed you."
You lift your leaves, deepen the green
Dance in the wind. Promise to survive.

Some deem you lowly. I rate you royalty
Remember the seven week drought—
With care I'll share your rooted shoots
Spread green beauty everywhere.

❧

The Cactus and the Rose

Arlene Spector

I planted a red rose bush;
At least, I thought I did.
I watered her and fed her,
and dreamt of many flowers.
I pruned and pinched and sprayed her
And softly whispered prayers.

"Oh God, please tend my rose bush.
Let her brilliant blooms delight.
Give her some thorns to protect her.
Give her sun and rain and light."

I watched and dreamt and waited
For my little plant to grow,
But I hadn't grown a rose bush,
And so, I couldn't know that
She wouldn't put forth roses
With just a few small thorns.

Instead, I'd grown a cactus
With many spines to wound,
But with rare and precious flowers
On a rose bush never found.

I've learned to love my cactus.
I tend her from afar.
I touch her blossoms gingerly
And keep her where it's warm.
I'm careful not to overfeed
Or come too near her spines.

But now and then when the sun is gone,
My garden in repose,
I close my eyes and remember when
I dreamt of a red rose.

చ

French Garden

Marie T. Dufour

I've tilled the soil
I've toiled the earth
With tools of steel
Or bare fingers.
Buried the bulbs,
Scattered the seeds.
I've fertilized,
      Insecticide,
      De-pesticide.
I've even, even killed your snails!
Cheri, mercy!
Won't you pity my dirty nails?

❧

Garden

Ruth Dement

A bright jewel in the heart of the city
A secret garden tucked away out of sight
Lush foliage of various greens
Sparkling colors, brilliant and breath-taking.

Old familiars in unusual colors
Exotics never seen before
Every color you can think of
And some you never imagined.

A secret garden hidden away
An enchanted spot
There must be fairies
Peeping out at you from under the leaves.

Here is a bench to sit on
To gaze in rapture at all the glory
Who would have thought that such beauty
Could dwell in the heart of the city?

જ

Rejuvenation

Ruth Dement

Slowly I walk along the street.
I ache and every step hurts my bones.
I loathe the cane—the necessary "third leg."
The wind blows my hair in my eyes.
I am irritable and cranky
And then I come upon a piece of magic.

A narrow strip of earth between cement and wooden wall;
Is burgeoning with life. Tall grasses
Make shifting patterns, golden arcs
Against the dark brown wooden wall;
And weeds, dark green swirls of leaves
Flat on the ground, send up slender stems
Topped by cones of buds, fringed at the bottom
By delicate miniature flowers,
Making a perfect Mexican Hat.

I smile at such charm in a mere weed,
My heart is lifted up by the beauty
Created in such a tiny place by accident.
How can I be grumpy when such magic exists;
When life will not be denied—
Will insist on occupying every nook
and cranny without encouragement or tending?

❧

Bonsai

Mary Freericks

You are trimming the maple
even its roots
till the leaves turn miniature
wiring its trunk.
The pot so small
you must water it
each day
and cut a willful branch
that shoots out
grows large leaves again
destroying
your work of art.

ↁ

Returning

Yvonne Mason

I roll tiny flat seeds in my fingers
Press the seeds into the ground
Anna's hummingbird darts the velvet
Sun center of the lone white daisy

I drop bulbs into their dark homes
Monarchs glint orange fast as a
Chorus girl kicks up her legs

I pick zucchini, tomatoes, corn, beans
Sunflowers spread their smiles offer
Striped teeth to diving bluejays

Basil drops all his leaves cherry
Tomatoes shrivel on the vine
Bromeliads go wild as the possum's
Frosty dew decorates my pines

Dreams of seed catalogues fill my head

This year's seed
Is the dream of
The flower, like
Music played outdoors

❧

Nature's Solace

Mary Cook-Lund

When I lose myself and wander off muttering
Let nature find me a place in her arms
Bundled up sitting on a rock in my garden
Balancing blackberry tea on my knee
When I yearn for sleep while still awake
Give me my memories, treasures and dreams
Set me in a pool of sunlit pebbles
Wash me in sand and time until clean
When I'm overly full of toil and turmoil
Let me see my reflection in a bird bath bowl
Float on the breeze that lifts butterfly wings
Open my hand to the beauty of life
And watch petals fall in the dust of the earth

❧

The Dahlia

Lilian Reshen

*W*hy did I fall in love with you, Dahlia?
Met you in the hands of a gentleman
    who grew you in his garden.
Brought you to the office to show you off.

I was amazed by your gargantuan size.
Spectacular color—vibrant purple red.
There are many species of you, Dahlia;
    but you are the most beautiful and
decorative; though you are hard to grow.

I know a little about you, Dahlia.
You were named after a Swedish professor,
    Andreas Dahl.

Raised in Spain, traveled through Europe,
    Mexico and are now in the Americas.
But, am unable to find you.

Came close to seeing you again, Dahlia,
    at Halloween.
The shape of a fan, pompon, mistletoe in
    reverse, paper pumpkin.

You will forever be in my mind.

❧

Reverence

Rita A. White

The flowers bend in
Graceful reverence
To His Majesty, the Wind.

ᘒ

FLORAL BOUQUET.

Roses 1

River Montijo

He always brought me red, red roses,
    a dozen longstems,
      showy, not fragrant.
Balancing their heavy, hothouse heads
    on smooth, costly stems,
They faded in a day or two
    from menstrual red to
      wilted, October maroon
And never unfurled their tight-coiled buds
    to burst into mature riot,
      petals flung and hips swelling.
Bound in adolescence, their promises decayed.

They cost the most, I know.

But, oh, for a sweetly spiced, stolen bouquet
    of sherbet-pink garden roses,
      short, woody stems buttressing cabbage
      blooms
As aphids squat between thorns,
    sucking sticky juices.
And the sun-warm smell of damp petals
    cast loose from ruddy hips,
Crushed to my nose
Or tucked into a private drawer
    filling that dark place with
      summer scent.

ɛ♉

Caretaker

Colleen Costigan Welch

Whose garden,
Blossom, bloom and bud?
Whose this beauty
That I care for like a child?
Tend, feed and water,
Trim and scold about
Bad friends — the weeds.
I say it's mine
And sometimes share
Its bounty with my house
And neighbors.
But when I'm in the garden
On my knees,
Surrounded by its beauty,
Oh, I know
Whose place it is!

❧

A Bumper Crop

Mary Blei

The tomatoes are a vivid red,
the corn stands tall and green.
The gophers ate the cabbage
and finished off the beans.

The carrots disappear…
d
  o
    w
      n
        w
          a
            r
              d
…at an alarming rate.

Because they eat fresh vegetables,
we've got the healthiest rodents
in the whole United States.

⁊

Field

Delane Morgan

Worm-level,
in a field,
survey the weeds:
rough stems,
pricked with want,
ragged leaves,
lace of summer suns
woven into the pattern
of Queen Anne
in the texture
of crocheted snowflakes,
thistles plunging
daggers into blue,
stabbing stars
in the early heavens,
the white moon low
in the day sky,
and the lowly milk weed,
with brown stems
and sticky milk pods,
blowing free to billow
cascades of jeweled snow,
cobweb feathered silver.

Celebrate beauty
with blossoming Queen Anne.

Defend the kingdom of the heart
with thistle.

But follow the way
of the milkweed.

❧

My Home

Jo Ann Schaefer

There is a place I love to go
To sit—be idle—and see my
  flowers grow
It has a fountain that sings
  a song
Vines and ivy are all around
Trees rustle in the wind
I sit and remember my
  childhood friends
There is no happier place to be
Than at my home with my
  cats and trees.

&

Wellspring

Muriel Mines

The blossom sprang from nowhere
unexpected, but delicate and pink.

The struggle to blossom at first faltered, then
by the bright sun, warm air, the wind and rain

The minuscule bud grew—slowly, steadily
though tossed about by storms and dry, hot summers.

Surviving, it burst forth and in time birthed other buds
whose colors carved a rainbow—tall and beautiful.

જ

A Bad Seed

Robin Wallace

They curse me
as a common slut
strutting boldly
in garish yellow
defiling their
pampered grass.

Never to reside
amidst angel hair,
baby's breath and
polished stones
breathing
lemon-oiled air.

Why should I care
when I've survived
their pronged blade
at my very root?

Before they snuff me out
my globe of winged seeds
will soon fly off
in vengeful procreation.

❧

Virginia Landscape

Carol V. Davis

Just once before I leave this Virginia landscape,
I would like to go into the fields at night.
The cows come to me, at first individually,
then in groups of two and three.
My arms wide, they circle me, click of hooves.
I do not see the swish of tail, but startle at
the cool breeze in the warmth of mid-May.
I stroke each blade of wild grass, committing
its sleek body to the memory of my hand.
Later the blue black of night sky rises,
pulsing like a jellyfish to the surface of morning.
Fog obscures the sun over the valley.
How difficult to leave the dogwood, the red oak
spreading the fingers of its leaves at dusk,
the moth who visits mid-morning.

❧

My Eucalyptus

Katharine vanDewark

I walked among eucalyptus groves today
                   bodies that shimmer
                         silvergraygreen and   soft a whisper
Copper brown skin   breaks   and blisters   across a branch
So flagrant in random composition   to sear   my eyes
                   yet I cannot turn away
Draw me in   closer   seduce me with your scent
   your delicate underbelly reaching
            languidly through space   yellow   air
Irresistible   I touch   so moist and dry
         smooth   pliant sinuous   a lover's arm

   Brilliant warm   translucent leaves meet in painful grace
         legato branchlets   adagio limbs
            cascade in tumbles over   spiral   twisting
trunk which then   EXPLODES its bark   into puzzle pieces
   layer and layer of subtle gauze   vibrant misty brown
   dusk cream rose and tan   breath of violet and orange   all
                all peeling falling away to reveal
                silver gray green and soft
         bodies that shimmer glow   murmur
You cover the ground with an oriental carpet of your leaves
   opal koi flash pink   palest tan and blue purple
         all the same   each different
      a mastery of subdued tones   hues unequal

Press my body into yours   dissolve
         into the whirling   reaching calm
         your clean and heady spice   Lend me
your spirit for a time and suck me in
            that I may know your silence static movement halted time
            bear the painful beauty   unendurable in my present state
Yet wait   wait through sunrise noon and set
         spring   fall summer night   October heat and
                vernal equinox   new moon quarter than full to half
Seeds fall scatter tossed across the ground
         invisible buds form appear tender green on branches
         acra russet   verdigris grow swell
         their breath contained within
a hard shell   turning smooth green   to knobby brass and bronze
            then burst forth   as fireworks through their cross

A lifeline to the tree shrivels   snaps They drop
Pure cycle renews itself   again   again

&

Two Ways of Looking at Petals

Delane Morgan

The Young Man:

"See!—the hanging basket there—
Why must the fuchsia spill its bells,
Profusion of petals in purple and pink
As wind its beauty tells?"

The Old Man:

"The basket sways, and petals swirl
Shadows on the window glass.
the chain twists, the fuchsia turns,
Snowing petals on the grass."

☙

Oak

Arlene Spector

Look at me and do not judge
By what's been written by time.
Look at me and see beyond
The scorched bark of ancient fires.
Within the gnarled and twisted trunk
The sapling lives and grows.

❧

Tassajara

Regina O'Melveny

Last night near Suzuki Roshi's resting place
the yucca plumes blazed with moon.
A single bat feasted
on the invisible life of the air.

Spirit is a pungent thing:
sage crushed underfoot,
feverfew brushed against the leg,
sweet bay laurel held up to the nose,
skunk musk in the meadow,
musty oak humus, fresh coyote scat,
dry hot earth under my fingernails.

This morning bees swarm
to the dusky poppies
and leave the yellow dahlias
all alone.

Hundreds of emerald beetles
stud the shadow side
of the alder trunk.
The tree, a queen
draped with bright insect life.

This year swimming in the creek,
I taste the drought
ending.

Electric-blue damselflies
light on my knee,
fluorescent twigs, globular eyes
which see everything
as they couple
and fly up twinned over the rushes.

Light on the creek
becomes water,
and water returns
the favor.

At night a cool speck of light
flickers on my closet door
then vanishes.
Glow-worm
spark cast from the green fire
of the forest.

෴

Tassajara is a Zen monastery in the mountains east of big Sur.

Dream 1

Carol Soucek King

Meet me down by the brook,
Sweet Breeze. You know my favorite nook
In the grasses that grow tall by my height's
Rock. Don't go one wisp further, Breeze,
For the water nips its passers-by
Just a foot away and would have
You rushed along with it. But stay
And stir the tall grasses in which I'll stand.
Stir, too, my thoughts. Cut their roots
And let them rise higher than
The grasses can. And let them ride
With you—my dormant thoughts.

☙

Fragrant Reward

Mary Lee Friesz

I pruned the American Beauty,
Gave the Tropicana one last spray,
Weeded beyond the pale Oregold,
Thought to fertilize another day.
All the while, I slowly watered and
Trimmed the flowing floribunda's hips;
Finally, over their deep-set roots,
I spread the protective cedar chips.
Before I quit the flower garden,
I plucked withered brown leaves from the ground
And gave a quick snip with my clippers
To thick jasmine growing all around.

Noting the luscious bedside bouquet,
A vase of red tipped Double Delight,
I claimed reward for my long labor:
The roses primly greeted our sight.
The jasmine trailed a profusion of
Tiny blossoms, a plump waxen white,
Out of control under the windows.
Tropical fragrance colored our night.

❧

Palos Verdes Spring

Arlene Spector

Coreopsis, mustard, heather, broom
Splash the hillsides
Light the gloom
A crazy quilt of gold and wine
Blankets the shore.

Wild fennel, jasmine, mint and gorse
Scent the windgusts
Chase remorse
June's misty gray
Enshrouds the cliffs.

Bougainvillea, begonia, azalea and aster
Nature's palette
Who can master?
Artists spring up like
Toadstools in autumn.

Wistful, moody, joyous, aware
Lovers pine
Their hearts to share
Spring has called
The young to mate.

Ain't it great?

&

Lost in a Wild Wood

Lydia Castilho

Lost in a wild wood
lost in its charms
singing of color
spinning a balm—

lost in its soft kiss
aromatic in flows
spilling a blessing
of bluebells and rose—

tulips and daisies
sigh as they nod
paving a pathway
the sleeping sun prods—

finding a true friend
you are this girl
lost in a wild wood
found in my world—

❧

Diminishing Returns

Dorothy V. Benson

I tried a winter garden,
gave it water, love and feed.
Carrots took eight months to grow,
and then they went to seed.

I tried a summer garden,
planted corn, cucumber, chard.
I'd beat the cost of living yet,
and daily worked the yard.

Now that we have cucumbers,
long waited and much prized,
I can purchase two for a quarter,
I've seen them advertised.

❧

Sedge

Regina O'Melveny

This particular afternoon
fills me with joy.
Alder branches dip to the creek,
tremulous flocks of dun-grey birds
feed on catkins and berries.
Sun suffuses the water.
A young sycamore
stands alone on the boulder.
Sedgegrass trails the creek
like the raspy green hair of witches
who love the changing element.
Their breasts are smooth granite.
Their sodden log thighs disappear
in the brown velvet
of creekbed detritus.
Like them I love the water.
My soft pink flesh, wispy hair
drifts with the current,
remains rooted in change.

Flowers

Anita Woods Vitro

Come plant a seed so it can grow
Quite lovingly tend what you sow
Make plans and worry, watch and wait
Beckon life into unknown fate.

Look, see it now
It's peeking through
So young and weak
So sweet and new!

Soon days will be forever changed
A life of dreams must be arranged
Love and care from a gentle hand
Bring flowers to life, pure and grand.

❧

Just Being Neighborly

Nan Sherman

Five petals of the white hibiscus
with its pale orange stamen, yellow pistil,
dance near the pink hibiscus
with its scarlet stamen and darker pistil
The white mimics a lily pad,
the pink, with its fluted layers, a rose.

Together, they are a skirt
for the holly tree
growing from my neighbor's garden,
towering over them,
its spread of leaves
green lace in the sky.
The border of flowering azalea bushes
growing below the hibiscus,
provides a ruffle for the skirt.

Branches of my pink hibiscus
bend over the redwood fence,
like a woman's arms
offering a bouquet,
decorate the neighbor's yard.

From the opposite side
flowering vines from another neighbor
circulate through the slats of our gazebo,
climb upwards and purple the roof,
an Impressionist painter at work.

Nodding and murmuring in the wind,
all the flowers, trees, vines
converse and conspire
to break down barriers
separating neighbors,
and bring closer together,
earth, sky, people.

೭ഠ

My City Garden

Colleen Costigan Welch

Come outdoors with me,
And see my garden,
How tenderly sunlight
Threads through leaves
And spotlights first
One flower, then another
There in the corner
The feathery fern,
An aging ballerina,
Nods in answer
To our adulation.
Out here no colors clash,
There is a harmony
Not found on city streets
Just steps away.
Let's stay here,
You and me,
Out in my garden.

❧

Mom

Lois Olsen

My mother embarrassed me so much.
A Gertrude Stein spirit,
she gardened in combat boots, no bra,
and "jeanies" from "Freddies."
She talked to me about tomatoes,
when I didn't want to hear.
Now, I grow tomatoes,
and garden in rafting sandals,
and nylon Nike shorts,
and embarrass my children.

Green Time

Delane Morgan

Into the sun-plowed dawn,

Out of the night,

With the burgeoning of green roses,

With the sap of green fruit,

Into the restless garden,

Out of the motionless shadow,

Come the green tendrils,

Like nebulous undersea weeds

Weaving the net of spring.

❧

Fall

Ruth Adams

Light changes.
Mornings are moist with fog that creeps above the hill
to chill our hearts. And yet
sometimes by afternoon a breeze like spring comes whispering
against our cheeks... the dreaded Santa Ana blows.
Gathering fury as it comes, it sucks the moisture from the air
and thrashes drooping peach and nectarine. Rusty leaves go flying.
Only the loony apple trees hold fast.
Towards the end of August they decided, inexplicably,
to bloom again.
Now, for the second time, jade-green marbles cling
in spite of devil winds.
We'll be eating fresh applesauce for Thanksgiving.

Asters and chrysanthemums are blazing scarlet, gold and amethyst.
the hummers feast among the sage's brazen purple spikes.
Flicks of movement where the tangerines glow orange assure us that
the warblers have come back.
It's time to sow against the spring's return:
Lupine and poppies on the wielding slope,
Onions, leeks and cabbage in the kitchen beds.

With any luck we'll soon be seeing rain.

☙

Digging for Dinosaurs

Carol V. Davis

In this time between seasons
when the sky refuses to abandon
itself to the summer sun,
I plant my garden, tuck the roots
in with the same care I use to pull
the quilts over my boys' legs.

The reassurance that it's always been like this —
digging in the redwood chips and mulch,
picking through the seeds,
like my friend who plants in oak barrels,
ever confident the steep sides will deter pests
or the woman in the next town
who waters every evening precisely at dusk.

Just now my son grasps
his orange trowel and begins to dig.
How I wish I could satisfy his needs.
We could find something — a few small bones,
not even white or smooth, a chip of skull.
What can I say when he looks up at me with
those believing eyes?

❧

Window Wish

Mary Cook-Lund

A wish for a window
Wide, open and tall
A view of the garden
And stone waterfall
To hear small splashes
Of baby birds bathing
See sunbeams stream
Through thick scotch pines
A white wood window
For wonder and warmth
To marvel the might
Of the natural world
Harmonies of beauty
And human design
Letting go the pretension
To claim it as mine
A wish for a window
Wide, open and tall
To let the world in
At its own beck and call

❧

My Terms—No Worms

Madge Dugger

Flutter by, white butterfly
Don't make little skips and stops
On my precious flower tops
If it's nectar that you need
Feed upon a flowering weed
You with dainty wings and legs
Go far off to lay your eggs
Those small dots will turn into
Worms that chew and chew and chew
So I mutter when you go by
Flutter by, white butterfly.

છ૭

Threshold

Edna Glover Mishkin

Not knowing where we are led, we follow
a shoe-hardened path meandering
half-mile from the woodlands above—
redwood, alder, pine families cohabit—
changing to brush, meadow grass at our sides
We stumble upon beauty unforeseen

Sandy beach haven
where remnants of loggers' harvests
lie vanquished, ancestors
of adjacent hillside sages, tree ghosts
recline in open graves, grouped mercifully
to commiserate with each other,
the wind, the sea and sun
Bled white some, gnarled the inners exposed
salt-washed, wind-whipped, silent
fragile in their nakedness

Plunged hip-deep
rock giants punch up steep from the sea cellar
dark rugged masses
against an uneasy fog—

The fog curtain just now
pulls up, barely time
for sun to lavish
an opulent embrace
Beach blushes rosy-copper
the cove trembles expectantly

Rolling crushing fireball
descends to shimmering sea,
liquid and undulating, the sun
shooting flame, the sea
Each dissolves in the other finally

The cove murmurs

> You have called me, my room
> my temple, counterparts
> down a dark corridor
> where I have stumbled
> but have found you
> choose here to dwell
> nor shall I wander far

❧

Wildfire

Arlynne J. Chevins

The wind whispered the secret,
The brook flaunted the tale,
The lilacs rioted on the hill,
The buds broke out of jail.

The scandal blazed from tree to tree,
The squirrels spread it shamelessly;
The roses blushed to see her fling
Herself at Life, that Madcap, Spring!

છ

Journey

Barbara Kovner

Shimmering trail of garden snail
Silvering up the path
Calligraphed curved loops and whorls
Framed with waving grass.

Messages like petroglyphs
Define space, time and place
Remind me of our tranquil walks
Through springtime morning's lace.

Glinting trail of new-formed life
Shared hands, shared hearts, one will
Subdued in evening's reaching dark
Now shadowed, gray: quite still.

ⅇⅉ

Black-Eyed Susan

Ann Bulloch Brown

Black-Eyed Susan, what do you see
When you look from your iridescent eye at me?
A middle-aged woman weighted by rue
Whose worry lines deepen as Time comes due.
While your corona of golden-sheafed corn
Waves at Helios early each morn
And you greet Dawn with a laughing eye
Apollo's little sun reflecting his sky.
You wink at my efforts so youthful to be
Oh, Black-Eyed Susan, help me to see.

❧

Sounds

Deborah Kotter

Birds rustling in bushes
Birds building in trees
Birds calling birds
singing words—SPRING.

❧

I Am a Leaf

Susan Salomon Neiman

I am a leaf falling from a tree
twirling in parachute circles to the ground
I am tree deep rooted in the earth
reaching to the sky
infinite and volatile
transparent and clear
opaque and unfathomable
black and bejeweled
rainbowed and inviting
I am the earth
hard and cold
arid unyielding
luscious and fertile
clothed in hyacinth.

I am a stream flowing
clear cool water
falling in cascades on mossy covered stones
rounded and smoothed by me
falling like golden hair
sparkling in the sunshine
endlessly pouring.

I am languid wisteria
drooping over weathered lattice
a pink calla lily
in a terra cotta pot
a hummingbird hovering
over life's sweet nectar
a million molecules
a single breath
an echo and an ash.

ॐ

Magic

Carol V. Davis

All summer I have waited
for the perfect time to plant corn
so it will rise up unaware of its
scruffy patch of earth.
Not like the failed sunflowers
blackened centers
even before the burst of seeds.
I had promised grandeur.
We would borrow a video camera
record the glory of six-foot splendor
send the tape to garden shows
make lots of money
buy a new house with a huge yard
where I would plant zucchini
that wouldn't rot mid-flower
tomatoes never annihilated
by demonic horned worms
and I would plant row after row of corn
eat it all summer long
letting fat kernels slide down my chin
then throw them in the air like confetti
to have enough, more than enough
even enough to waste

❧

Martha's Garden

Nancy Warder

I always plant posies between the vegetable rows,
Cosmos, pansies, nasturtiums, marigolds
It does a body good to see them bloom.

My red and roughened hands are never still
Chopping wood, kneading bread, building fires,
Washing clothes in the old tin tub, feeding chickens,
putting up fruit in glass jars.
When I stop to read the Bible by lamplight, I sew
at the same time,
Fine stitches that hold quilts together.
The devil finds work for idle hands to do.

My nearest neighbor's light is five miles away.
Twelve children, seven of them lived.
The rest lie buried yonder on the hill.
I always called my husband Mr. Crawford, never
by his first name.
When he died, I could scarce remember it.

Here in the sagebrush land you can see for miles
to the pale mountains.
In the afternoons, the wind rises and the tumbleweeds
roll rustling against the fences.
There is no one here but us.
My nearest neighbor's light is five miles away.

I always plant posies between the vegetable rows,
Cosmos, pansies, nasturtiums, marigolds
It does a body good to see them bloom.

ℭℐ

At Chumash Point

Mary Freericks

Painted suns bloom
from their shoulders.
Lightning zigzags black
across the nipples
of the young braves.
They are red winged
black birds. The sun
epaulets, the lightning
feathers, black as emptiness
before any breath,
red as the fire of life.
Their arms lift,
the shells bell the deer skin.
The cane of the mother wears the skin
of a rattler,
carves the earth.
They drop seeds,
sage sprouts, a Chumash garden
blossoms above the cliffs
and the ocean smiles
dolphin tales.

☙

Weed Therapy

Susan Norton

There's something quite healing
About squatting down into the soil,
Digging deep with trowel or gloved fingers,
And pulling out wild invaders of our garden patch.

Sometimes, they protest too much,
And grab hold of Mother Earth so tightly,
Extra human effort is needed
To rid them from their tentacled nest.

Other gardeners might complain,
But for me, this is a prescription for mental health,
Removing all the pains and problems past
With each volatile pull.

At the end of a successful day of weed wrestling,
My back may hurt, my shoulders complain,
But the pressures from a harried life
Are somehow wiped away by this therapeutic tug-of-war.

❧

My Garden

Peggy Baumeister

My thumb is not exactly green;
My gardening talent is in-between.
A flowering triumph—an ego pump
A futile failure—a total slump.

The first, a yearning to be proficient,
Capable and most efficient.
Every seed that I plant does well,
With flowers that have a tale to tell
Of perfect sowing, food and such—
It's plain to see I've learned so much.

The second is, alas, more real.
No matter the amount of zeal
With which I try to do each chore,
I probably could have used some more.
The weeds immune to every science,
Show remarkable defiance.
The aphis make themselves at home,
On my lovely roses they happily roam.

My garden never will be Versailles—
Blue ribbons surely will pass me by.
But I don't care one little bit,
I find such utter joy in it.
Working with my seeds and sod,
I feel so very close to God.

❧

Lynn's Moonflower

Lois Olsen

Waiting, waiting
for a moon flower vine
to grow,
so I can watch its
Blue flowers bloom
to the sun's set.

ಌ

Daffodil

Deborah Kotter

In the garden I was the first
Of early spring, the one to burst
My ripened bud and show
A golden flower to the sun.

But winter crept back into spring
Its icy wind whipped everything
And now I'm first to rest my head
Upon the lawn.

৵

The Jacaranda

Madge Dugger

"You'll be sorry if you get that tree,"
My husband warned at the nursery
"Flowers are messy—it's deciduous
The neighbors will soon raise a fuss
Our yard is small, where will it fit?"
I listened naught and purchased it.

While packing soil around its base
I whispered, "Hide that ugly place."
For years I had a secret goal—
to rid the sight of a telephone pole.

In spring the branches all were bare
No shade so tulips blossomed there
And when they faded right on cue
A purple tree burst into view

Later falling petals made
A carpet of a wondrous shade
A multitude of fern-like leaves
Now shimmer in the summer breeze
How beautiful! No pole to see
Oh how I love my "no-no" tree.

ཀ

Of Patterns in Trees

Lydia Castilho

Etched against the sky
contrasting dark on light
in motionless display
a fine and wondrous sight—
tiny ferns—

of myriad lacy fronds
or jagged branches bare
like swiftly running cracks
impinging on the air—
in patterns—

all shadowy here and there
sharply pointed spires
of needles bushy, full
like thorny twigs of briers—
one discerns—

in startling difference palms
with shaded bands of arcs
scalloped edging the sky
in semi-circled marks—
of patterns—

ल

Palos Verdes Sun

Lois Knight LaRue

Warm tendrils caressing the sere earth
Calling to the deep seeds asleep
Come, awake, arise, grow, stretch, rejoice;
The sound of the turtle is heard in the terraced land
Heralding renewal in the springtime of Life.

Garden Boxes

Lois Olsen

We have garden boxes that have no garden in them.
They overlook the ocean, and we enjoy the view.
Once they were overflowing with zucchini, corn
and strawberries —
we looked forward to the harvest.
Furry visitors arrived in moonlight,
the raccoon, the fox and skunk,
the greedy critters feasted
on all within their reach.
From our garden boxes
we enjoyed four strawberries.
We have garden boxes that have no garden in them.
They overlook the ocean, and we enjoy the view.

❧

Monterey Pine

Wanda VanHoy Smith

Wind-shaped pine trees of Monterey.
  If trees could talk, what would they say?
Their giant cousins grow
  Far from the shops of Cannery Row.

In back of gas stations and motels.
  Across asphalt lots of big hotels
Behind thick bougainvillea covered walls
  Find an oak tree where a song bird calls.

Duck through a secret door
  Into a garden you've known before.
Blushing ivory roses climb
  Around a window into time.

Flaming red geranium flirts
  Bright as señorita's skirts
Line paths where Robert Louis Stevenson walked
  Where the author and his true love talked.

Did they breathe the roses' sweet perfume
  While finding treasure in an upstairs room?
The wind-shaped pines of Monterey.
  If they could talk, what would they say?

❧

Exotica

Robin Wallace

My
winter garden
quiet brown and dormant
in the chill stillness,
except for the steam
rising off the fecund heap
where early this morning
with pitchfork I pierced
the icy needled hoarfrost
awakening an army of detritivores,
beetles and mites digesting
chopped prunings and citrus rinds,
leaves of comfrey and feverfew
jagged shards of egg shells
and coffee grounds from Costa Rica.

Burrowing below,
squirmers recently imported
from the Nile River Delta;
their plump pink bodies gorging
on spiral-peeled pippins
crunchy pine needles
carrot crudités
curls of radiccio,
and tooth-scraped leaves
of Jerusalem artichokes.

Their distal ends ooze
strings of dark crumbly loam
earthly mysterious humus to feed
my expectantly resplendent summer garden.

ೲ

Sea Cliffs

Mary Crandall

Glistening golden mustard growing wild,
Shifting in the wind.
Piercing incandescent sunglow
Resisting forceful strength
Glances off periwinkle lupine,
Tips each fury-whipped wave
With froth of sprinkled glitter.
Fields of grasses sway, iridescent,
Silver-grey to wind,
Gleaming green to sun,
Hugging roots to earth for warmth,
Yearning toward the sky.

❧

The Cutting Garden

Lois Olsen

My mother started gardening after all her children left.
Out of shale she made a garden of stolen slips and cuttings,
clipped and slipped into her purse,
kept in a little nursery off the kitchen
until they were ready for the big beds of the garden.
It took thirty-five years to bring it to maturity,
and only one day for a buyer to make an irresistible offer
that ended the gardening, and left the gardener
to enjoy its beauty from afar.

☙

Lighting the Lantern

Regina O'Melveny

One summer evening in the canyon
I light the lantern,
and see night fall for the first time.
The silence that settles
after mockingbirds, woodpeckers, and jays,
before nightjars, owls, and crickets.
The moment the day's heat withdraws.
The still radiant ovens of granite.
The emergence of snakes and bats.
The smell of sage cooling down.
The darkening alder, willow, and oak.
The hush that empties us
in readiness for dreams.

☙

April

Inge Knapp

In Easter finery
dazzling, frilly white
Geraniums
party in my garden.

Spring breeze swaggering
petal flutter yellow
Poppies
lavish their charms.

Starry blue-eyed
sun sky mirrored, shy
Wild Iris
smile up at me.

❧

Garden Hoe

Marie T. Dufour

*W*hen evening came and brought him home to my garden
He stood squarely, boots apart on the brick-red brick.
The finch on the Chinese vase ceased his cheery chirp
And stood still on the limb of an orange blossom,
Sentinel to the mulch, perlite and potting soil,
Where entrenched tulips and croci await the sun
Beneath purple Johnny-Jump-Ups.

He snickered. From an empty pot—Terra Cotta—
My hoe's upturned claws fired a warning salvo.
Predictably, his index finger pointedly
Outlined the do's and don't's of agronomy,
Cursed the baffled pottery with sterility.
At last, Authority spun his heels on Botany.
And the Johnny-Jump-Ups perked up.

సౌ

Haiku

Deborah Kotter

The boy picks a pod
from our pale leafed tree, launching
seeds into the wind.

———

Tiny hummingbird
you hang at roof's dripping edge,
taking a rain bath.

ও

Spring

Ruth Adams

The sun has climbed the ladder of the days towards another equinox.
Sly fingers of its warmth
are prying at the golden buds of daffodils.
But hummingbirds are tiny balls of fluff
hunched against the winds
that like cascades of milky glacial melt
surge through bare branches.
Only the apple tree pledges tight pink buds to summer's warmth.

Halfway down our hill
the kitchen garden calls.
Time to uproot the last few straggling broccoli, to turn the soil
stirring up earthworms' lair, and sow our bean rows.
Then in a week or so we shall exult
to see sturdy green arches thrusting through the black
and know for sure that winter comes no more this year.

❧

WITH THE COMPLIMENTS
OF THE SEASON.

The Garden

Susan Jones

I look upon my garden blooming throughout all the seasons
and see daffodils in the spring bursting forth with delicacy,
greeting the springtime with blossoms anew.

Summertime roses, in a kaleidoscope of colors, climb
trellises and fill the air with fragrance so sweet showing off their
beauty all during the day and into the night.

Then, hummingbirds visit the trumpet vine seeking nectar
from blossoms growing brightly like a neon sign and
butterflies hover around the flowering jasmine.

In the fall, stately chrysanthemums appear with
hues of autumn blending in with the leaves on the
trees affording me beauty beyond belief.

And then in winter, with snow on the ground,
I see in my garden green foliage sprouting, and here and
there a rose or two sparkling in the morning dew.

How I love my garden in spring, summer, fall and winter
With a variety of plants and flowers growing beautiful and free.
The joy of seeing my garden grow means everything to me.

അ

Autumn From My Porch

Joan Forman

Butterflies flutter in among splashes of color—
where tall strains of red, yellow, and white roses bloom,
and fuchsia hibiscus flowers nestle in a green hedge.

A neighboring fir tree sways in a dance with the breeze;
its pointed leaves cling—unwilling to let go—
resisting then yielding to fate.

A splintered wood railing edges the porch where I sit
lit by the sun overhead at mid-day, warming me
while I contemplate the mellowness of the season.

Roof tops brush a cloudless blue sky—
grey gulls fly in from the sea nearby to perch on
telephone wires struggling for prominence.

I become absorbed with verdant and transitory images,
merging them into deep recesses of memory and self,
the grandeur of life abundant and surrounding me.

A magnificent display spreads from sky to earth
obscuring inevitable regeneration and growth
ceaseless in a continuous cycling of life.

I learn from what I observe of nature in autumn,
mimicking the stance of a fir tree, dancing with the breeze,
shedding yellowing shrivelings of the past, to grow.

As autumn becomes colder, foreboding winter, I may not linger as long
to watch tree leaves fall, blossoms wither, seeds scatter,
life depart its worn shell to emerge refreshed in the spring.

Each autumn builds upon another, and as it fades into the past,
I augment images I have captured from my porch—
Sometimes I need to remember life's lessons.

❧

Eucalyptus Against Blue Sky

Mary Crandall

Tumbled brown earth to satiny grass
Twisted with roots.
Humps of root to silver-brown trunk,
Solid and smooth.
Trunk to limb
Limb to branch
Branch to twig
Twig to stem
Stem to leaf.
Leaves atuft,
Clutches of lacy spring green
Scattered with red.
Orderly progression
From roots in solid ground
To delicate tracery in the sky.

ε∂

Promise

Marilyn Norma Limond

Next year
I'll buy a small house
with a huge garden
where grass grows
green and lush
flowers overflow
hiding walkways.
Yellow roses, purple lilacs
white daisies, pink petunias
vie for attention.
Bird feeders swollen with sunflower seeds
peanut-butter treats
invite robins, cardinals and chickadees that live out back
in pink or white dogwood trees
pines, to come and feast.

I know I'll find this place
where I once lived
away from city sirens
and screeching traffic

where quiet grows tall
skies stay blue
birds serenade
crickets harmonize

and love fertilizes
all living things
making them grow.

My spine straightens—
My spirit heals.

&

To The Insects in the Garden

ellen

I like how your little mouths
suck the Catalina currant
and the lemonade berry

how your tiny whisker-legs
climb the Indian fig

how your faerie wings
lift you from the half-leaf
of the lilac

how the cluster of black dots
tells me where you've been

❧

Terpsichorean Trees

Madge Dugger

They glistened in their finery—
The Pepper wore her Spanish shawl
Jacaranda was in lace
At this dancing costume ball
Eucalyptus sleek in simple sheath
The classic style she took
Crape Myrtle's ruffled blossoms
Flounced the feminine look
Fringed needles shimmied the Charleston
Pine tree's skirt was green
Cottonwood wore cotton
Jazzed up in bright sateen
Swaying, twirling in the breeze
All in the finale bowed
Their rhythmic dance was perfect for
The men were not allowed.

❦

Garden Scents

Lydia Castilho

Soft is the scent of blossoms
touched by a sunlit breeze
sweet as a sugared stirring
of childhood memories —

swift as a swallow calling
o'er the crest of trees
drift to a land where rainbows
dwell in the breast of peace —

where in the whispering sunshine
other days have sped
where speak the leaves to petals
in other garden beds —

seek there the love and caring
the promises made and meant
found in the smile of friendship
cradled by the garden's soft scents —

❧

Legacy

Barbara Kovner

Sweet Sabbath comes for me
      the day I contemplate creation
      while digging deep to essence
      with spade and searching trowel
      intoxicated joyous inhaling
      earth's rich aroma
      embracing my infinity:
      this force-field is my home
When first I started gardening
      three generations past
      my sharp-edged blades
      of pruning shears in
      autocratic thrust
      would snip: cut: hack: destroy: remove
      all brown stiff dying twigs
Inevitably time beckoned me
      long years consumed my youth
      my flashing blades
      chose subtler paths
      my heart a wider truth
While planting my small universe
      I patterned your patient guile
      your wisdom nutured growing seeds
      benevolent the while
Each newborn generation seeks
      life-giving light: its style
      determined measurably by
      mature ordained conception
      draws strength soul's shape
      deft harmony for
      future's warm protection
Deep roots inseparable: entwined
      reach newfound depths unknown
      communicants of age-old truth
      defined by heart-felt home
Your source your spirit's
      thrusting blooms
      continue now with me
      and with our child and with his child:
      nature's subsidy.

છ

in your branches

Marlies Schmudlach

Silence is your voice.
your leg will never run.
your water-filled pipes suck the dirt.
our mothers are not one.

your breath saves me from death.
and without my air, you could not breathe.

we are colored and bent unlike the other,
yet our paths follow a similar course.
we bud.
we grow.
we die.

nature's hard afflictions have chilled our structures.
you tremble—
stripped of your protective coat.
i tremble—
exposed during the inspection of a lover.

most walk by and only imagine
a fire, or boat they could build with your parts.
even though we are like fraternal twins,
they only watch the pictures that dance inside their head.
ignorance clouds their vision
of the reflective mirror
in your branches.

ೞ

Nightgarden

Sandra Benat

*A*n early moon, high and full, winks
at Venus, a white moth flutters between
the bushes, the cats run around the clay
pots on the deck; the sound of distant
laughter passes by.

The air is perfumed with lemon and
rosemary, grey sage and yarrow; they
whisper among themselves, compare
scents. The portulaca glistens in its red
wood container, the grapefruit tree silently
bears its fruit; the lily is already asleep; an
old verbena stooped by its own weight, sighs.

I sit on a wrought iron chair, feet up on
a mosaic table I made to sell but didn't;
a glass of sherry in my hand, fragrant
and smooth, slips down my throat; in my
head I hear music, pale and foreign, try
to remember where I've heard it before.

The evening pauses; I step onto the still
warm brick patio. The cats have settled
into one deep breath, the moth has
disappeared, the music has stopped.
In the sky, gigantic galaxies of dots swirl,
the universe explodes. In the garden, I
am overcome by sleep, stumble into the
house. Inside, I close the glass door, lie
down on the bed, fall into a wordless sleep,
dream of rain.

❧

Inner Well

Mary Cook-Lund

I sway to the rhythm of the aqua sea
In a sisal net of memories and salt air spray
I dance in the forest of the softest moss
Barefoot and free in a whispering breeze
I linger a while in a sun filled meadow
Rolling in clover and Queen Anne's lace
I rest in the arms of a tangelo tree
As white cloud clusters collect in blue sky
I hear my own heartbeat from the wellspring of nature
And listen with wonder, respect and devotion

❧

Dream 3

Carol Soucek King

Hold me tight, oh garden scene,
Don't let me miss a single thing,
Not leaf or flower, so fresh and clean.
Oh, nuturing earth, teach me to dream!

The breeze enlivens every path
By gracefully swaying the fountain grass
And acacias' masterly rhythmic stance.
Oh, gentle wind, teach me to dance!

The mockingbirds high do beckon me
With joyous notes while soaring free
In melodious flight throughout the spring.
Oh, wondrous choir, teach me to sing!

Infuse my spirit. Erase my cares,
My thoughts too filled with doubt and fear.
And bring them back to me refreshed.
Better this day than years of rest.

Hold me tight, oh garden scene,
Oh nuturing earth, teach me to dream!

For the Orchard

ellen

Consider the Beverly Hills apple,
how it doesn't need frost
and how its bare twigs
like the ribs of an Asian fan
grab a surprise thick rain
in desert air.
Consider the way the strength of its bark
protects unseen buds,
and how we hunger for its fruit,
as a rare tropical lightning storm
brings more humidity than is natural.

***

Garden in a Box

Susan Norton

For some,
    their gardens grace acres.
Mine is confined
    (rather succinctly)
        to wooden boundaries
that fit a shelf above my kitchen sink.

There it rests,
    an abridged arboretum,
Its walls compactly fence
    the blossoms
        within
while keeping insects and soap suds
        without.

It sits
as regal as any formal garden,
    lush
        verdant green
            punctuated by brilliant blooms.
Lilliputian lumber borders
    do not intimidate its growth
        or dim its flowered hues.

Though its size in measure may be small,
    the moist aroma
        of flowers mixed with detergent
floods my senses
    and my caretaker's heart.

❧

Poetry Seedlings

Wanda VanHoy Smith

There is nothing so fine
as standing in golden sunshine,
blowing fluff from a dandelion.

He loves me? He loves me not?
Is it crazy
to ask a daisy?

෴

Biographies

ADAMS, Ruth. Her poetry has been featured in magazines and she has also published a children's book. She is a member of a local writer's group and lives in San Pedro.

BACHAR, Jacqueline. Editor/Publisher of *Poetry in the Garden*, she is a former Associate Editor of an area publication. She currently is a Contributing Writer for a local magazine and the author of *A Collection of Letters From Mary Lott to Deacon John Phillips, 1826-1846*. She is working on a biography of Elizabeth Cady Stanton. She is a resident of the Palos Verdes Peninsula.

BAUMEISTER, Peggy. A former professional singer who appeared under the name of Peggy Laurence with the Eddie Duchin band, she has written poetry since grammar school. She has four children, five grandchildren and three great grandchildren. She lives in Beverly Hills.

BENAT, Sandra. She enjoys gardening and poetry about gardens. She has published in poetry journals and is currently working on a book of prose poems about life in the suburbs. She lives in Torrance.

BENSON, Dorothy V. Former Editor and Secretary of The California Writers' Club which was formed in 1909, she is a prize winning poet and short story writer. Her work has been published and she is currently working on a novel. She resides in Berkeley.

BLEI, Mary. She is a free-lance writer who lives in Torrance. She is a member of several writer's groups. Her articles have appeared in national magazines and local papers. Her short stories have won prizes in writing contests and will be published.

BROWN, Ann Bulloch. She has received several awards for her work from among others, Writer's Digest and the Sacramento Writing Competition She's a former Script Analyst for Turner Network Television and teacher of English and Creative Writing. She resides on the Palos Verdes Peninsula.

CASTILHO, Lydia. Born in Hongkong, she has been published in several books and will have a piece in an anthology of the National Library of Poetry. She lives in Torrance.

CHEVINS, Arlynne. A former employee of the Department of Defense in the Pentagon, she writes poetry, articles, fiction and non-fiction, "ad-infinitum." She resides in Torrance.

COOK-LUND, Mary. A university professor, she had two poems published in *Beautiful Gardens* magazine and will be published in an upcoming book. She lives in Lomita.

CRANDALL, Mary. In a request for a biography, she responded, " I have no bio. I am elderly. Sometimes I write poems which I hope are poetry." She is a resident of Rancho Palos Verdes.

DAVIS, Carol. A resident of Los Angeles, she has published in several magazines and anthologies.

DEMENT, Ruth. A resident of Albany, she has been writing poetry for two years. A former Licensed Vocational Nurse, she is actively involved with Older Women's League.

DUFOUR, Marie. Born in France, she has been a musician, song-writer and singer. A grandmother, she now consecrates her time to writing poetry, and the study of prosody. She resides in Huntington Beach.

DUGGER, Madge. A member of a local poetry group, she resides in Rancho Palos Verdes. An active volunteer with the United Nations Association, she received recognition for outstanding voluntary service to that group. She enjoys nature and up-beat poetry.

ellen. A resident of Malibu, she received the 1995 Gennaro and Theresa Iodice Award for the best poem on the Italian theme. She has had hundreds of poems published in books, journals and magazines.

FORMAN, Joan Faith. A free-lance writer and seminar leader, she has worked as a public relations manager, contributing editor, and columnist. She was named Woman of the Year by a local aerospace corporation in 1989. She lives in Redondo Beach.

FREERICKS, Mary. Published in anthologies and magazines including *Cosmopolitan*, she was a recent winner of the Allen Ginsberg poetry contest sponsored by Passaic Community College. She was also awarded a poetry fellowhip from the New Jersey State Council on the Arts. She teaches poetry in Santa Barbara where she resides.

FRIESZ, Mary Lee. A Phi Beta Kappa graduate of the University of Arkansas, she had her first poem published in the Arkansas Democrat in 1958. She has been published in newspapers and an anthology. She resides in Rancho Palos Verdes.

GREENSTADT, Emily. A ten year old student, she lives on the Palos Verdes Peninsula. She's in the Girl Scouts, plays piano and enjoys sports. She is a semi-finalist in the National Library of Poetry competition.

JONES, Susan R. A former Federal government employee, she has published a volume of poetry. Her interests include poetry, singing and word games. She lives in Long Beach.

KING, Carol Soucek. The former Editor in Chief of *Designers West*, an interior design magazine, she has published several books relating to architecture and design. She was named Woman of the Year by the Network of Executive Women in Hospitality and currently lectures in architecture and design. She lives in Pasadena.

KNAPP, Inge. She has published a book containing poems, pen drawings and songs, and has recently completed a biography of her mother. Born in Germany, she lives in Santa Barbara where she enjoys hiking and nature.

KOTTER, Deborah. She began writing when her first grandchild was born. Her children's picture book received an award from Please Touch Museum for Children in Philadelphia. She's a member of several writer's groups and enjoys gardening. She resides in Culver City.

KOVNER, Barbara. A former teacher, she has five grandchildren. She has previously worked in public relations. She has been writing verse since age eight and is a current participant in a Poetry Workshop for Older Women. She has been published in the National Library of Poetry. She lives in Glendale.

LARUE, Lois. Upon her graduation from Marymount College in 1968, she received the Dockweiler Gold Medal for excellence in all liberal arts. A resident of Rancho Palos Verdes, her writings have been published in various newspapers.

LIMOND, Marilyn Norma. She has published many works in children's magazines as well as newspapers. She is listed in *Two Thousand Women of Achievement* and currently writes poetry and children's fiction. She lives in Marina del Rey.

MASON, Yvonne. A former California Poet-in-the-Schools, she is currently a Food & Travel Editor. She has been widely published throughout the country and has won prizes for her visual art as well. She enjoys her herb garden at home in Manhattan Beach.

MINES, Muriel Newman. An active volunteer, she lives in the Fairfax community of Los Angeles where she has been recognized for her work with older adults. A resident of an Alternative Living for the Aging, she has receieved a commendation from Mayor Tom Bradley for her research work on the 1985 Fairfax Mural Project.

MISHKIN, Edna Glover. A former actress and creative drama teacher, she helped to form an Equity-waiver company and theater in Burbank. She is a member of the National League of American Pen Women and has received recognition from them for her writing. She lives in Pacific Palisades.

MONTIJO, River. She began writing as a teenager and produces poetry and short stories, receiving awards in both fiction and poetry. She lives in Hermosa Beach.

MORGAN, Delane. She has written several hundred poems; about ninety have been published. She published a book on the Palos Verdes Peninsula and has written book reviews and articles. She takes animal portraits and plans on a book combining both skills. She lives in Redondo Beach.

NEIMAN, Susan Salomon. She is a psychotherapist and published poet. She combines writing and therapy in an on-going workshop and believes in the healing power of nature. She lives in Los Angeles.

NORTON, Susan. Her poem, The Poet was read at the National Poetry Day Festival in Rockport, MASS, as a winner in the National Poetry Day Contest. She was Editor's Choice for Outstanding Achievement in Poetry-1995, presented by The National Library of Poetry and her work has been featured in several publications.

O'MELVENY, Regina. Writer, assemblage artist, teacher, she has been widely published. She won first place in the John Foster West Poetry Award and second place in the Arizona Authors Contest. She lives with her husband, daughter and many animals in the coastal sage-scrub hills of Rancho Palos Verdes.

OLSEN, Lois. Published for the first time, she belongs to a poetry reading group on the Palos Verdes Peninsula where she lives which she credits as the "source of the ideas" for the poems. The members are Barbara Smith, Ann Hugh, Pam New, Joan Kelly, Carol Ronlof, Lynn Gecks, Janet Behrendt, Gail Allen and Susan Hernandez.

REAMES, June. She is an Air Force wife and is currently attending college where she majors in Art History and will work toward a Master's degree in Library Science. She is publishing for the first time. She is a resident of San Pedro.

RESHEN, Lillian. She started writing poetry in a class at a senior center. She does the newsletter for the writing group to which she belongs. She lives in Los Angeles

SCHAEFER, JoAnn. A former nurse, she enjoys gardening and belongs to a local garden club in Rancho Palos Verdes where she resides. She is publishing for the first time.

SCHMUDLACH, Marlies. She works as a VISTA (Volunteers in Service to America) leader with the California Conservation Corps. She resides in Sacramento.

SHERMAN, Nan. Her poetry has been read on PBS and her poems featured in several publications. She's a former actress and recently retired from the National Council of Jewish Women's Center. She resides in Los Angeles.

SMITH, Wanda Van Hoy. She has published children's and young adult books and articles for children's magazines. She also published a series of career booklets, as well as a young adult horror novel. She lives in Hermosa Beach.

SPECTOR, Arlene. She wrote her first poem at six, sent it to Eleanor Roosevelt and received a letter of appreciation from her. A former teacher and community college career counselor, she currently participates in public poetry readings. This is her first publication. She lives on the Palos Verdes Peninsula.

SPEEVACK, Yetta. A resident of West Hollywood, she saw her first spider plant in Puerto Rice where she spent time after winning a Ford Foundation scholarship. She is the author of a children's book called "The Spider Plant." She currently lectures in schools on children's literature and is working on a poetry cookbook.

vanDEWARK, Katherine. She began writing in a group led by Regina O'Melveny where she was introduced to "wild writing," a method "rich, revealing and enjoyable." She has also performed as a supernumerary with the American Ballet Theatre. She enjoys life on the Palos Verdes Peninsula.

VITRO, Anita Woods. A former school teacher, she now works as a writing aide. She has published in journals and also privately published a personal poetry collection. She calls the Palos Verdes Peninsula home.

WALLACE, Robin. She is a free-lance writer, artist, poet, registered nurse, frustrated gardener who resides in Nevada City.

WARDER, Nancy. Born in 1921 in Oregon where she grew up, she has worked as a union organizer, social worker and ceramic artist. She began writing ten years ago. She resides in Oakland.

WELCH, Colleen Costigan. A former newspaper feature writer and teacher of creative writing, she started writing poetry three years ago. Her work has been in several publications and she is a member of a poetry group who reads in local coffee houses. She lives in Manhattan Beach.

WHITE, Rita. A resident of Los Angeles, she spent her early years as an Air Force brat. She worked for a newspaper doing weekly columns and feature stories. Her work has been published in newpapers, magazines and anthologies. She is currently with a production company in Beverly Hills.

❧

Index

By Title

By Author

ORDER FORM

INTERNATIONAL FORUM
P.O. Box 7000-350
Palos Verdes Peninsula, CA 90274
Tel: (310) 377-2339
FAX: (310) 544-6015

Please send the following book(s):

Poetry in the Garden
ISBN 1-886934-07-x (hard cover), at $19.95 each

NAME _____

ADDRESS _____

CITY _____ STATE _____

ZIP _____ – _____

TELEPHONE (_____)_____

Shipping & handling:
Priority mail: $3.25
Book Rate: $2.25 (Surface shipping may take three to four weeks)

_____

Quantity _____ x $19.95 each $ _____

Plus 8.25% tax for books shipped to California addresses _____

SUBTOTAL _____

Plus shipping/handling (see note above) _____

TOTAL Enclosed $ _____

Please make check for the full amount, including shipping/handling
(and sales tax for CA residents).
Make payable to: INTERNATIONAL FORUM.
Send to the above address.

Trade discounts extended to book dealers, wholesalers, distributors.
Please contact International Forum for information.